THE VALUE OF PROCESS

When Destiny Meets Reality and Reality Became Her Testimony

Lori A. Manson Futrell

ISBN 979-8-89345-670-7 (paperback)
ISBN 979-8-89345-671-4 (digital)

Copyright © 2024 by Lori A. Manson Futrell

All rights reserved. No part of this publication may be reproduced, distributed, or transmitted in any form or by any means, including photocopying, recording, or other electronic or mechanical methods without the prior written permission of the publisher. For permission requests, solicit the publisher via the address below.

Christian Faith Publishing
832 Park Avenue
Meadville, PA 16335
www.christianfaithpublishing.com

Some names have been used others have been substituted for the purpose and the writing of the book however all statements are true and correct.

Printed in the United States of America

DEDICATION

This book is in memory of and dedicated to my dad, Vincent John Yade Sr., who went on to glory on December 6, 2005, at the age of seventy-six. I so wanted his approval all my life.

In a visitation from the Lord prior to the writing of this book, my dad said, "Preach the Word, Lori, and continue to teach, train, and transform the lives of people. Lori, I am so very proud of you, and I love you. As I sit here with the Father, I am forever watching over you."

To me, that was the completion of the beginning of this great journey for the Lord.

This book is also dedicated to my mom, Elaine Ann Grunert, who also believed in the call of God on my life.

Who entered Glory the early hours of May 22, 2024 she was ninety.

ACKNOWLEDGMENT

I first want to thank my Lord and Savior, Jesus Christ, for saving, blessing, and keeping me.

To my children, Auther, Shannon, Asa, and Savannah, for loving me unconditionally through the mountains and valleys of our lives and now for the work that God has called me to do.

To my brother, Vincent John Yade Jr., there were times he did not understand my journey, yet he never stopped loving and believing in me.

To my friend, Sheila Perry, who has always believed in me even when I didn't.

To my sister in Christ, Mia Richmond, who saw me when I never could see.

To my sister, a true friend who has walked with me through the years, the mountains, and the valleys, Lisa Henderson. Words can never express the support and love she has for me. I am so thankful to God for her.

To a good, good friend and a former pastor of mine, David Amos, formerly the founder of Hosanna Christian Center, who taught me the value of simplicity.

PURPOSE

The reason and purpose for writing this book is to tell the entire world that there is a plan for your life. No matter where you are or the type of family you come from, you might have come from a broken home, a two-parent home, poor or rich, no matter what state of mind you are in. Boy or girl, man or woman, married or single, it starts here. Functional or dysfunctional, always remember this.

Jeremiah 29:11 states, "For I know the thoughts that I think towards you, sayeth the Lord thoughts of peace, and not of evil, to give an expected end."

The value of the process is seven simple Kingdom principles to daily Christian living. I promise you that you will enjoy reading it and it will change your life forever. If God has done it for me, he will do it for you, for his promise is yes and *amen*. God has given you a vision and a purpose, and today is a brand-new day for you. So now, reach out in faith, grab hold of my hand, and step into your destiny. We will and can take this journey together.

So are you ready? Let's step.

CHAPTER 1

In the Beginning, I Prayed

I asked God where I should begin, and he said, "Go back to the beginning." I got saved at the age of thirty. I was pregnant with my second son, my third child. My daughter Shannon was my second child; she was born out of wedlock and was a convenience. I got pregnant with her just because he had pretty eyes, so we made a baby. No job, no stability, just pretty eyes. Satan will try to keep us blinded if he can; the trap was already set by the enemy. Prior to getting saved, I had been shacking up for almost one year. I got married in September of 1989 and accepted the Lord Jesus into my heart in March of the following year (1990). At that point, I knew my life was going to change forever. God had to do a quick work in me; I had to grow up fast. I knew that God had a plan for my life and my journey was just beginning.

Jeremiah 29:11 tells us, "For I know the thoughts that I think towards you, saith the Lord, thoughts of peace, and not evil, to give you an expected end."

I was married, or so I thought, to the greatest man in the world. We had a dream wedding. Everything I prayed for, so I thought, was coming together. I was looking good; I had lost sixty pounds; you could not tell me anything. I just knew I had arrived. How many of us today are living just like that? We say quotes like, "It's okay, cool, it's going to be fine, I don't need any help, I got this," and the whole time you are drowning in your own muck. I gave birth to my son, Asa, on September 12, 1990. Shortly after that, the dream wedding ended in divorce.

*"But they that wait upon the L*ORD *shall renew their strength; They shall mount up with wings Eagles; they shall run, and not be weary; and they shall walk comment and faint not" (Isaiah 40:31).*

I should have waited, if only I had taken the time to pray. God was nowhere in that I was the one in control. I made things happen for me, *not God*. It was all about me. My ex was a closet crackhead. Every day I would come home, and piece by piece, things would be missing. There were sometimes days, even weeks, he would never come home. He would take me to work pregnant, told me he would see me at the end of the day, just to leave me sitting with no ride. I would fear the car leaving. I would go to sleep with the car keys and the money in my sock under my head while I slept. Everything I've worked for was slowly disappearing. My dream wedding, my home, my so-called happy life was slowly coming to an end. I began to pray prayers of desperation: "Lord, help. Lord, deliver. Lord, drop him dead. Just release me from this hell that I am in."

I have learned over the years in the Christian journey that we must pray always, seek God for everything. Allow God to lead you; after all, he knows what's best. What father leads his children astray? Will he put them in harm's way? No, he would not.

Obedience is better than sacrifice.

Had I only taken the time out to listen and pray?

CHAPTER 2

God Had Redeemed Me

As the journey continued, just shortly after my first marriage ended, there was still a plan for my life. My first home. I worked for a small hospital in Stamford, Connecticut; it was called Saint Joseph. I was again single, raising my three children Auther, Shannon, and Asa. Things for me were now looking pretty good. I was approved for my home on $8.50 an hour, no money down, and bad credit. God is a super big God. I then moved to Bridgeport, Connecticut. The house was in the heart of the inner city, drugs all around me. *The devil had a trap set.*

All my life, Satan has set different traps for me to be deceived or get tripped up, these I called rabbit trails. God sets the course and the path; he gives you an instruction manual called the Word of God; he has seen the end, and he knows your future. Yet and still, some of us hardheaded people love to explore. Mama says no, we say yes; God says to wait, it's not good. We say I'm going to find out for myself. Hardheaded folks. I would be going along well for a while, and suddenly, a rabbit trail in the form of a brother with a form of godliness. He was always less than me. If they spoke a little Jesus, that was alright with me. I would say, hey, he's workable.

Mr. M, they called him Jazz. He talked about the game; we communicated by way of collect calls and letters for about six months. We got married; he was fresh out of jail, that was his fourth bid, he was to be released on parole. Little did I know, he was a drug dealer. All in one night, in a matter of minutes, my life was headed into a downhill spiral straight into the belly of hell, into the hands of the enemy. My older son, Auther was taken from me, and placed in juvenile detention, my two younger children, Shannon and Asa, were placed in foster care. I stayed in this mess for almost three years. Every day I would come home from work and walk on eggshells, not knowing what to say or what to cook that night.

> For God had not given us the spirit of fear but of power in a love and a sound mind. (2 Timothy 1:7)

He was not only a drug dealer; he had become addicted to drugs, the ones that he supplied. I had become codependent; I would go and purchase his drugs as long as he would stay home with me. I was active in church, Miracle Faith World Outreach, with pastors Bobby and Chris Davis. I would go to church like nothing was wrong, always smiling. He was in and out of jail; it had become a revolving door for him. Every time he was released, I was there to pick up the pieces. I would always say, maybe this time, God, it will be better.

Well, he never got better, only worse. Jazz beat me almost on a daily basis. I can remember one evening he came home from a drug run, high, drunk, and not alone but with another woman. I remember cooking a really good dinner that evening, only to get slapped in the face with it, kicked in my ribs, punched to the floor, only for him to say, "Get up and clean it up. Get up and take a shower, wipe those tears away, and come to bed. I'm sorry, let's make love." I felt so violated and dirty. I am the youngest; I have an older brother. I could not even tell my family about the abuse; I was so ashamed. My only hope was in God. I can remember sitting in church one Sunday, praying.

THE VALUE OF PROCESS

This was my prayer: "Lord, I know that you blessed me with my home. After all, Lord, it's not mine anyhow; it belongs to you. Lord, I can't do this anymore. I am not safe; my children are not safe. If you tell me to leave, give it all up, I will just go. Lord, deliver me from the hands of this enemy." In an instant, I heard the Lord say, "Sell the house." So I went home, called the realtor, and in less than one day, the home that had been placed in my hands had sold. There was still yet a plan for my life. God had not forgotten me. In April 1998, within thirty days, this sale was finalized. I can remember the day we prepared for relocation; Jazz came to the house, stood with a gun to my head, and said, "If you leave, I will kill you. You will die this day." My words were, "I would rather be dead in Christ than to live in hell with you." He turned and walked away. In May of 1998, we arrived in Memphis, Tennessee.

God hears your prayers, despite your disobedience. My prayer for today, for the one that is being abused: God loves you. He did it for me; he did not call you to that lifestyle. You are not to be violated anymore. You are a chosen vessel by God. Get out now. Trust me, take the first step. God will open doors that you could never imagine, close the old one forever. God is no respecter of persons; if he did it for me, he can do it for you.

Be it unto you according to your faith, and take the first step.

> Then he touched their eyes, saying, "According to your faith be it done unto you." (Matthew 9:29)

CHAPTER 3

I Had Become an Overcomer

I had relocated to Tennessee; things were once again going well. I had my two younger children; my oldest was still in Connecticut in detention. God had blessed me with a good job once again. New city, yet no friends. I had a native family, a God sister from back in the day. It was new to me; I could not adapt. So what did I do? After nine weeks, I later packed up my children and hooked up a U-Haul trailer to my snow-white five-speed Ford Explorer. I had told the children the night before that vacation was over, and we ran back to Connecticut to the familiar, my comfort zone. Only to realize upon arrival, it was not my home anymore. My home was sold; I had to take a two-bedroom apartment in the inner city. My oldest son was still in detention. I conceived my last child, my youngest daughter, Savannah Faith. We lived in the inner-city apartment for four months; my son was released from detention at the age of sixteen. Only to return to Memphis, it was January of 1999, this time with my three children and my unborn child.

At that point in my life, I was so not ready for another child. I was forty, and once again, I began to get back on course. I could remember praying one day, "God, take this child from me; let me abort naturally." Shortly after arriving in Memphis in January, I got a call from my mom that my Nana had died; she was ninety-three. My mom was devastated, and I began to hemorrhage. The bleeding would not stop; I was rushed to the hospital. Her biological father moved to Memphis with us, only to leave one month later. I could remember being at the hospital; the ultrasound tech ran an ultrasound, her little heartbeat, it was so strong. I was twelve weeks pregnant, for him to only say she would abort naturally; there was nothing they could do to stop the bleeding. I was later released to go home. I could remember praying to God, "Why are you allowing this to happen to me?" His reply was, "Was that not your prayer request, daughter?" He said, "I could take it away if I choose."

He then replied again and said, "Daughter, I will not honor that petition. She will be used by me; she is my chosen. She will do great things in my name. Just watch, wait, and see." Savannah Faith was born July 30, 1999. Then I met Nikki, another trap set by Satan. He was twenty-one; talk about Stella getting her groove back. This time it was Lori getting her groove back. He talked a really good game; before I knew it, we were married. The day of the wedding, I could remember after the fact, and saying to myself, "Lori, have you lost your mind? What were you thinking? Have sex with him, even have an affair, but not marry him. You really did it this time, and now, you're stuck and have to deal with the roller-coaster ride, and it's going to be a trip." I was married to one of my children; my children even acted more mature than him.

God had opened another door for me to purchase my second home. The church I had attended with Nikki had shunned me because I would not listen, even though the warnings were in front of me time and time again. I did not listen, so they just pushed me aside instead of loving me. They never prayed; they never even listened. For a period of one year, I had drifted into the wilderness. I can remember one day my God sister calling me and saying, "Her name was Christina, most of us just called her Chris. She said, 'Come with me to this cool church. I believe it will bless you.' She said, 'You have nothing to lose.'" So I attended; that was in March 2001. At that point in my life, I began to fight back, take my life back; this time, I was doing it in the Word of God.

In April of 2001, during the Easter Sunday service, God called me into the ministry under the direction and teachings of my pastor, Tim Vandouser. My life was in turmoil, yet and still, God had a plan. I was consistent in church, very active; I taught Christian education. I began to seek God more and more. I had a really good job; I worked for Methodist Healthcare Business Office. My spouse was still acting crazy. Women were calling my phone, and he would stay away each day. I did not want to work. He had abused me mentally, which is worse than any physical abuse. I used to pray, "God, will you just let something happen to him?" or "God, maybe he will just disappear forever. God, just let him drive off a cliff, please." It had become a joy to go to work. I hated coming home, only to face his stupidity. My children started to hate him. Toward the end, he began to use drugs. Yet I was getting stronger, and God knew what was about to take place. I can remember going to work daily and taking all the important information with me. Daily, I would keep it at my job in the event of a tragedy; it was a safe place. Little did I know, God was preparing me for my final release.

On March 4, 2004, I woke up; this day was different. My spouse had not been home for five days. I went to work only to receive fifty-two phone calls that day. That was the day I told him it was over. No more was I going to take it, no more was I going to be abused. On the last and final call, my response was, "When I get home, you're to be packed up and gone. Get out, it's over." I left my job that day, looked at my boss and my coworker Kim, and said, "Pray for me, someone is going to die. I can and will not go through this anymore." I drove home only to find his stuff still there. I packed it up, drove it to where he was, dropped it off, only to see his face in fear. My response to him was, "Trash belongs with trash; you will no longer have a home anymore." While driving home, I noticed that he was following me. I arrived in my driveway; he was behind me. Once again, he was in fear; the devil was upset with me. He picked up a brick, smashed the windshield of my minivan; glass shattered all over me. Then, he came to the driver's side window where I was sitting; with that same brick, he smashed the window, only to hit me on the left side of my head.

I was stabbed in my left shoulder, kicked in my ribs, bleeding, and left for dead. My children came out of the house and ran. It took the EMS team one hour to arrive that day. My cell phone was ringing, only to hear, "I am going to come back and finish the job." I was later rushed to the hospital. This was on a Tuesday. I can remember being treated in the hospital, and my two friends, Lisa H and Lisa S, one white and one black, both holding me, one on each side, and Lori in the middle, crying and saying, "It's over, you have been released."

In the wee hours of the following morning, I was released from the hospital. That was on a Wednesday. I can remember going to church that evening and praising, standing, and rejoicing that it was finally over. I thank and praise God for my sister in Christ, Lisa S. She made me promise to spend that Wednesday evening. It was like a calm before the storm; it was so quiet. Something was about to take place. You see, he did come back to finish the job in the early morning hours of that Thursday morning, at 4:00 a.m. We received a phone call that my house was firebombed, and the point of impact was my bedroom. Lisa Stafford heard the voice of God and saved my life and the lives of my children that evening. I will forever be grateful for her and her obedience to the Lord.

Listen, wait, and obey the voice of the Lord.

CHAPTER 4

Totally Committed

I could remember driving from Brighton to Memphis between 4:00 and 5:00 a.m. shortly after a call came into me. With my baby and my oldest child, Auther, my middle children were with church friends in safety. As I was driving, I said to God first, then placed a call on my cell phone to my longtime friend and coworker, Kim, and said, "That fool firebombed the house. Everything is gone, destroyed." She kept me on the phone that morning; it seemed like the longest drive. The faster I went, the longer it took. She said, "Don't be shocked, the spirit is telling me it's all gone." I turned the corner to Genyth Avenue. All I could see was fire engines lining the whole street from one end to the other. The house was gone, only one corner beam had remained; the bedroom I slept in was disintegrated.

When dawn came, the fire chief had released what was left of the house back to me. I could remember walking through a rubble of smoke and ash, only to look down at a piece of my Bible, a corner of the page burned on one end, sitting at the top of the ash. It was as if God himself placed it there for me to see (the words said, "Love thine enemies"). I was in awe. I stood and looked at my children, hugging and holding each other in a circle, crying as I watched and realized it was all gone. The remnants from my past in Connecticut were gone, burned to ashes. I then said to God, "Now what are we to do, and where are we to go?" His response was, "I am getting ready to do a new thing in you. Watch and wait and see, but most of all, I need you to trust me." By this time, I was committed to him.

God was so good. When I purchased the house, I had no idea the type of insurance I had purchased in the event of a fire or tragedy. I never knew the limits, and less than one day, $3,000 was placed in my hand, then months in the mail in abundance. We checked into a hotel; my children shopped till they dropped. You see, prior to the fire, it was all about Nikki; my children suffered for years. If not him, it was another man in my past. The men got the best; my children got the leftovers. Now, it was all about them, at least so I thought. I could remember getting a phone call in the hotel room where I stayed, and on the line, it was my friend Laurel. She said, "It's your time now. This is your season. Go forth and start preaching." *Let me leave this footnote with you: it may be your time but not your season.* It takes years of preparation and preparing. We then moved into a rental house. I then began to go ahead of God; my foundation was not solid. I was not even healed from the wounds and the scars from my past.

Most of my sister friends in the Lord said, "It's time to preach, tell your story." It was in April, shortly after the fire, I met Catherine Burks. She was the founder of Women on the Frontline for Jesus, and she was Laurel's friend. She would have prayer once a month in her upper room; the women would meet, pray, and talk about the third heaven experience. Wow. I could remember my first meeting; I was so fragile. I knew nothing about ministry, all I knew is that I was called. I can remember sitting on the floor, and Catherine asking me to share. It was then *PROCESS* was placed in my spirit, less than a five-minute message. That's when I really began to go ahead of God; it was my time now, so I thought. My children were suffering; they had been crying out. I never saw the signs. My daughter Shannon had slipped into the spirit of lesbianism; my oldest son was having an identity crisis. Juvenile detention caught up with him; the demons from the past had become addictive, the spirit of pornography hovered over him. My younger son stood alone, quiet and separated; he took care of me, my little girl, his baby sister.

On October 28, 2004, my divorce was finalized, the third and final time. The next day, the twenty-ninth, we closed on our third and final home in Millington, Tennessee. For years after that, God kept me hidden. I was active in the church, consistent with Women on the Frontline. Catherine had begun to mentor me. I stayed close to her for a season; she loved my children. Art had moved out. Shannon had dropped out of school; she was out of control. Catherine had given me the opportunity to preach in the Washington, DC, area. By then, Shannon had enrolled in Job Corps. While on her break, she traveled with me to DC; that was the last time I saw my daughter somewhat whole and complete. I believe she took the trip just to make me happy. The title to my message was *"When Your Back Is Against the Wall, Turn Your Face to Jesus."* Little did I know I was about to take a turning point in my life. Shannon never returned home. Shortly after, I left the front line; all that was left at home was my two younger children. The house was quiet, and I was finally at peace. It was me and Jesus.

CHAPTER 5

My Life Was Everlasting

The house was quiet; there was a peace in the air. I had begun to attend Bible college at my local church, a satellite branch of the North Carolina College of Theology. All I did was study and work. That was a time in my life where I walked closely with the Lord. I can remember my first year of college; it was December 5, 2005. I was at work when the phone rang; it was my brother, telling me my father had taken ill. My world began to crumble. That was on a Monday. I was to attend Bible college that night; it had begun snowing in Tennessee.

One year prior to that call, my dad had come to stay with me from Thanksgiving to New Year's. That was in 2004. Prior to that, I had not seen my dad for five years. I naturally assumed my dad would live on forever. I can recall one Sunday morning prior to Christmas, Brother Jesse Denton and I, with the help of the Lord, led my dad to Christ. That Sunday, he accepted the Lord Jesus into his heart; my dad was seventy-five. He returned home that January 2005. During that year, we had made plans for my dad to return; he was going to live with me. I thought there was more time; little did I know, he would never return. God had a greater plan.

I can remember standing in Bible college that evening, in the midst of a snowstorm. The class was canceled, but some of us yet still showed up. I began to share with my brothers and sisters that my dad had taken ill and it was not looking good. I needed to leave on the next flight to go home. I shared with them my flight was leaving the next morning. We stood, and we prayed that evening. I recall saying, "Lord God, if you take my dad now, it is well with me. But Lord God, let me see him one more time." The next morning, I got to the airport; my flight was delayed due to inclement weather conditions in New York.

While waiting at the airport, I received a call from my friend Catherine Burks. She said, "Lori, nations are about to change." At that point, I had no earthly idea what she was talking about. My flight left Memphis after being delayed one hour, to only arrive one hour ahead of time in New York (now that was nothing but a move of God). There was a shuttle limousine waiting for me, took me to the door of the hospital. I walked in, and my brother was standing with the doctor; it was 2:00 p.m. I had not seen my brother in seven years. The doctor said, "Lori, I believe your dad is waiting for you." She said the night prior, she whispered in my dad's ear and said, "Your daughter is on her way." Remember, the night before, we prayed, and God honored and heard my prayer.

I can remember saying these words to my dad, "I'm here now, Daddy. Vinnie is here, standing by your side. It's okay. You can now go. We are going to be fine. Your grandchildren are going to be fine as well." I said it again, for the third time. That third and final time, my dad entered glory; it was 2:40 p.m. No greater gift. You see, one year prior, God allowed me to lead him to the Lord. He died at the age of seventy-six; that was on December 6, 2005. I remember calling home to my children, only to let them know that their granddaddy had gone home to be with the Lord.

To be absent from the body is to be present with the Lord.

> We are confident, I say, and willing rather to be absent from the body, and to be present with the Lord. (2 Corinthians 5:8)

THE VALUE OF PROCESS

I spoke to my oldest son, Auther. For him, his world was stripped from beneath him. Later that evening, my son went into the recording studio (creating a song entitled "Dedicated to My Granddaddy"). It was for all those that had lost a loved one. You see, it's never too late with God. You know it's your season and your timing.

Nations were, in fact, changed that week. That was another turning point in my life. I had begun to heal from the inside out. No more would I fall prey to the traps of Satan during that week. While visiting with my brother and planning for the funeral, the words came to me again nations are about to change. You see, while in flight, I had remembered something that had lain dormant in me. It had been blocked for thirty-nine years. At the age of seven, my babysitter's husband had been molesting me. This had gone on for months. I could remember him taking me into a dark basement for months and doing this to me. He would sit me on his lap, fondle and rub me, and molest me. I was so fragile and timid, and he violated me.

I can remember God saying to me in a small still voice that he was going to be there at the visitation. The night before my dad's funeral, not many people were there. It had begun snowing. My mom came. Frank was there, he was next to enter the room. Then there was M and Mr. D. You see, I was no longer that little girl. I was now mature a woman of God, chosen and set apart by God for the Master's use. I could recall Mr. D putting his hands on my face and saying, "You're still the same sweet, pretty little girl." I then leaned to whisper in his ear, "*I remember.*"

I turned, walked away, and began to greet others who had come to pay their respects. The priest had come; my brother was of the Catholic faith. His name was Father Joseamino. I remember him saying in a brief sermon to the family, "The only way to enter into glory is through Jesus."

The next morning was the funeral. Once again, it had been snowing all night. Only immediate family was there when we arrived at the church. Mr. D was waiting. The family then entered into the church. It might have been a Catholic Church, only to hear a

Christian message. When it was over, we assembled to leave. At that moment, I asked the funeral director to give me a moment.

I began to walk down the center aisle of the church, Mr. D by my side. He walked with me; he had his arms wrapped around my waist. "I am now a mature woman," I recall the words. "Bae, are you okay?" My reply was, "Yes." I then looked into the eyes within that two-minute window God has given me and said, "Mr. D, I am a minister of the gospel. God has called me. He's chosen me for ministry. I love you, I forgive you, but most of all, God loves you too. It is okay." That day, Mr. D was released from all those years of guilt and shame; he too received Jesus that day.

I hugged him, never to see him again. We drove to the cemetery; it was a forty-minute drive due to the weather conditions. We arrived at the Gates of Heaven, Valhalla, New York; it was still snowing. As I sat in the limo on the drive, I could feel all the shame and the weights of my past begin to lift off of me. I was then set free. When we arrived at the plot, we did the graveside ceremony. It was covered with snow, and all of a sudden, the snow stopped. I looked up, only to see the sun shining through the cloud, rays of sunshine. That was God letting me know he is with me and it is well. At that moment, I began to hear singing within my soul, "It is well, it is well, it is well in my soul." I was released from all of that guilt and shame. The sun was shining on me.

You see, it's never too late to have everlasting life.

CHAPTER 6

The Final Sacrifice

Upon returning home from my dad's funeral, I was a changed woman. I left Memphis broken and wounded, only to arrive healed and set free from the scars of my past. I still attended Bible college; I was still in the first year. I was asked to write a thesis about the journey. That summer, I received my associate's degree in theology. The following summer, in 2007, I received my bachelor's degree as well. Work was going well; children were doing fine; still involved in ministry, I had become content.

"You can never be just content when it comes to God," I could remember walking through my home with such peace and quietness. I was saying to the Lord, "Is there something more? God, you are the driver; what is my destiny?" Little did I know that evening, God was preparing me for what was to take place in the months to come. I would be making the final sacrifice. Yes, there was a greater destiny, and the Holy Ghost had become my driver.

I was later released from my pastor; my seven-year season had ended. He had released me into the hand of the Lord. He was confident that I would do well he knew the calling on my life, but he could not hold me back. Where I had served for seven years, there had been certain bylaws put in place. This was called tradition. I was a woman set apart and chosen by God with a unique anointing.

For a period of one year, I had begun to travel locally, visiting churches. I would enter certain churches, only to be called out, asked to take their platforms—not God's platform. These were false prophets. The Bible clearly talks about false prophets in the last days. *Matthew 7:15 tells us, "Beware of false prophets' power which come to you in sheep's clothing, but inwardly they are raving wolves."*

Remember, I was previously released by my pastor, and he was confident in me, yet I had no covering. The anointing on my life had become prostituted by these so-called prophets that would pimp me for their glory and advancement, not God's glory during this. I had begun to get scared and wounded in ministry.

While in this season, I was attending Hosanna Christian Center. Pastor David Amos, he invited me to come. He said, "Mom, don't be so quick to get involved. Just allow the Word of the Lord to minister to you. Sometimes we need to just sit and listen for a season." Remember, that first Sunday, I just sat in the back of the church, watching everybody, trusting nobody. When the service ended, my son introduced me to the copastor. He looked at me and said, "Prophet, God is calling you to a higher plane."

We attended for the next six months, God had begun to heal the wounds, and I began to get involved in ministry. One Wednesday night during Bible study, the copastor called me out again and said, "Prophet, God is going to use you to rebuke prophets. He is going to take you high in ministry; you will sit in high places."

Shortly after that, God chose me to minister to the people, and the title of the message was, *"I Have Anointed You to Preach the Gospel."* You see, that night, God was reaffirming my calling to the ministry. People had been pulling on me to the point of me being weighed down with burdens of many. They were trying to skate in on my anointing. Many looked at me. They looked at the prophecies and thought I was a fortune teller. "My God, what were they thinking?" None of them knew how to call on God. At that point, God said, "Enough is enough."

In April 2008, God began to speak to me and say, "I need you to leave it all behind. Leave the house, leave it behind." I said, "Well, God, if you gave me the house, and if you say leave it behind, that's fine with me." *No matter what happened in my life, despite it all, I always trusted God.* He said, "I am sending you to Houston for a two-year season." Prior to that, I had developed a friendship with a former mentor, pastor friend, and his wife; they lived in Houston. Months prior to that, God had been dealing with me.

He said, "I'm getting ready to do a platform shift. I'm going to deal with leaders first. I am raising up a remnant to take their place."

My son Asa just completed the tenth grade. School was not benefiting him; the teaching curriculum was not good, and he was dyslexic. I was told that the schools in the Houston area were far more advanced, and it would be a good place for him there, my daughter was living in Kentucky at the time. God was preparing me for the journey. On May 19, 2008, my daughter's twentieth birthday, I began visiting with her. That was when the devil detoured me for the last time. You see, I was delivered, but yet and still, I was not set free. I was still attracting younger thugs. After that weekend, I had returned home. God said, "Houston." I said, "Kentucky." I then began to question God. Just prior to that, God said, "I'm sending you to the land full of milk and honey." Once again, God said, "Houston." I said, "No, I'm going to Kentucky." My daughter was there, along with her friend and her brother, who had become my lover. Myself and my children left our house, job, and detoured to go to Kentucky. I was so hardheaded at the time. I thought if I could have my daughter move in with me, along with the others, I could do the saving. Not so. God does the saving, and I am not God.

On June 26, 2008, I preached at a youth revival in Memphis, Tennessee. Later that evening, God literally took his hands off me. Everything I've preached against, I went and did. For the next twenty-seven days, I would spiral into the belly of hell. God was sick of me. I had been preaching, coming home, and living a lie. How many preachers today are doing the same thing and still are (*wolves in sheep's clothing*)? There was a major pull on my life. Satan knew the future; he also knew that he needed to destroy me because I was about to shut him down. God had placed a mandate on my life. People wanted to skate on my anointing. I was tired of jumping, shouting on Sunday, and living a lie on Monday. Remember, the gifts and calling are without repentance. Yet I was living like a heathen.

God was fed up with me; he was sick of me. When I say he took his hand off me, he did just that. Never make Daddy God angry. His wrath, you do not want to deal with, period. Trust me, I know; I've been there. It seemed like the more I cried out, the more he allowed Satan to whip the mess out of me. While in my twenty-day hell season, I called my former boss at the old job. Remember, I had just left Methodist less than thirty days prior. I could still be rehired; my job was still open. I could go back home like this never happened. It was just that simple. No, not so. God had closed all doors on me. I had nowhere to run.

I had begun to cry out, "Lord God, where are you? I repent, Lord. I am sorry. Again, where are you, Lord?" In that still second, in a quiet voice, I heard, "Didn't I tell you to go to Houston?" On July 23, we packed up the house with the help of my two younger children. My mom, she has always been there for me. She never could understand why I did the things I did. All she knew is that I had a relationship with God, and I listened to his voice. The house was a rental property. I asked my daughter if she wanted to come with us and that she no longer needed to stay in that lifestyle. She chose not to go. My heart was devastated. I kissed her goodbye, wiped her tears, and we were headed Houston-bound. That was on the twenty-fourth. I drove a truck; my mom trailed behind me with the Charger. Once again, we were on the road for Jesus. This time, the path was correct; no more detours for me.

Remember the children of Israel, forty days in the wilderness? Well, for me, twenty-seven was enough. Unbeknownst to where we were going to live upon arrival, all I knew is that I trusted God, and there was a plan in place for me. While en route that first day, I received a call on my cell phone. It was the manager of the reserve at Tranquility Lake, fifteen miles south of Houston and currently in Texas. She said she had received a referral from a friend of mine. I was approved for a two-bedroom luxury apartment, and it was waiting

THE VALUE OF PROCESS

for our arrival. You see, God had already put a plan in place. But I chose to detour.

You see, back in 1998, I ran back to Connecticut. It was a two-bedroom apartment in the inner city with my two middle children. This time, upon arrival was ten years later, a two-bedroom in luxury from the glory of God. Yeah, climbing higher in Jesus.

This was the beginning of a two-year season of final sacrifice for me, two years of teaching and submission. We arrived on July 26, 2008.

CHAPTER 7

It Was Grace That Saved Me

We arrived in a new city; I knew no one, only a former friend, a mentor some of us called him Pastor Nolan. He had a very small church establishment. I was all alone with my two little ones. I had attended the first Sunday I arrived; it was so many miles outside of Houston. Shortly after that, we experienced Hurricane Ike. I will never forget it, plus it was my son's sixteenth birthday, which was September 12, 2008. Again, I had once started to question God with words like, "Lord, did I miss it again? Did you bring me here to die?" At that point, I was standing at the crossroads; this time, I could not tuck tail and run. You see, in the past, I would always run back to what was familiar. Not this time; I had to weather the storm, however long the season, it would be. I had to deal with it. God was not going to allow me to run anymore. He said, "You will ride this one out; there are some things that I need to teach you."

I never did return to that church again; he was another one of the wolves in sheep's clothing. God had allowed me to see that quickly. Around the corner from the complex, less than a five-minute drive, was Silver Lake Church. It was really a church that went beyond just Sundays. Pastor Reginald Devaughn was the senior pastor; the vision was restoring families one by one. God had a plan, and it was just for me.

Just as Jeremiah 29:11 said, "For I know the thoughts that I think towards you, saith the Lord, thoughts of peace, and not of evil, to give you an expected."

One of the neighbors in the complex shared about the church and invited me. Since I was at a crossroads of my life, why not? It couldn't hurt. She kept saying, "It's a good church. Visit with me." So I did. It was a Tuesday night Bible study. The following day, I received a message from the copastor saying, "Minister, is there anything we can do for you? Just give us a call; we are here for you." That, for me, meant a lot. I was hiding in a new city, all alone. The following Sunday, I visited again. Oh, and that friend, the one who invited me, she had joined, and she dragged me up front just for support.

As the pastor walked the line and greeted all of the new members, he stopped at me, and I said with a loud voice, "I am not here to join, sir." God did allow me to prophesy into his life. I also asked him to pray for me. I was still yet searching. I began to share that I was tired of pouring out and being abused. I needed to just sit and eat from a higher table. I looked into his eyes that Sunday, and he knew exactly what I was talking about, and he nodded yes, with tears in his eyes. Then, I said, "Pray for me." You see, he was going through something similar; he was beginning to get tired as well.

The following Sunday, Silver Lake became our church home. The restoration and building up of the family would take place there. Asa started a new school, Glenda Dawson High School, located across the street from the church, and he would be the first graduating class to take place. Who would have thought "ONLY GOD?" This was good; he began to come out of his shell little by little. He was adjusting. My little girl, she was also adjusting; for her, it was really easy. I had begun to realize that God was giving me a second chance to get it right. You see, I had made lots of errors with my older two, yet in still, God is able. Not thirty days after arriving in Houston, I was offered a job at Saint Joseph Medical Center. Talk about a full circle. My journey began in 1990 at Saint Joseph Medical Center.

God said, "I had to take you back to the beginning to show you where you missed it."

I now had a good job. Asa was in school, and little Miss Savannah was adjusting just fine. I was one of thirty-one ministers serving under a pastor, a church of seven thousand large. I began to see things through prophecy but could not say anything. Father was teaching me total submission. For some of us, that is a very hard task. Amen! The first year in Houston was a struggle for me. I had begun to cry out, "Why, God, do you have me here? You said milk and honey. All I see is deep waters." Desperation had begun to overtake me. I had begun to drown. I started to take my eyes off God and started to look at the situation. That was not good. The Bible teaches us to walk after the spirit and not after the flesh. *Romans 8:4 says, "That the righteousness of the law might be fulfilled in us, who walk not after the flesh, but after the spirit."*

God began to deal with me, and the teaching began. He said, "I have in the deep to teach you to float and be weightless. Just trust me; you will need to be light where I am getting ready to take you." I can remember looking in the mirror one day; no more did I see a wounded, ugly, scared woman. I began to see what God was seeing. THE SCALES WERE LIFTED FROM MY EYES. I saw beauty, and I knew I was perfectly, fearfully, and wonderfully made in the image of God.

Psalm 139:14 tells us, "I will praise thee; for I am fearfully and wonderfully made: marvelous are they worth; and that my soul know it right well."

The following year went by fast. Just prior to the season ending, I remember God saying, "Your training is over; you have been released."

I said, "God, what training? I am really doing nothing much here concerning training, only devotions and prayer, and to me, God, that's not training, that's habit. Oh, and on the first Sunday, communion. So, God, what training are you talking about?"

He said, "You're a mother. You have passed the test. Your foundation is now strong and complete. Your family is now restored. I am well pleased with you. Your released, you can go home now." (Home was Tennessee.) I learned a valuable lesson: *you can never go ahead of God.* My son Asa graduated on the eve of June 4, 2010. Early the next morning, on the fifth, we traveled home to Memphis, Tennessee. At this time, there was a house on a corner lot waiting on our arrival. Just prior to leaving, I wrote my pastor a heartfelt, somewhat personal letter. This is some of what I shared.

Dear Pastor,

>When I arrived at the lake, this prophet was broken and wounded. That family was so out of balance, no value at all. Your teaching, loving guidance has restored me. Pastor, you have no idea the people you can reach. I praise God for you, and I pray for your continued success. Remember to keep the flame burning; the fire of the Holy Ghost will never fail. This prophet is now complete, whole, restored, and healed. God has placed a mandate on my life, and my ministry waits. I am going home; God has released me. I will forever remember, love you, and miss you always. You will always be in my thoughts and prayers. I will never forget this experience; it has been a privilege and an honor just to sit and heal.
>
>Always in his grace,
>Prophet Lori

God can and will do just what he says. All we need to do, which is the key, is to trust and obey him. His Word will never return to us void. He is the same yesterday. He is the same today and forever. If he says it, then that settles it.

CHAPTER 8

The Last and Final Trap Set

July 14, 2017, seven years after the completion of my first book, and only book so I thought, I could never understand why my book was never published until this point. My phone rang, so I thought, the man I prayed for so many years ago. I thought he was my husband. You see, I had known him for ten years; he was a preacher, a cousin of a friend of mine. She was considered my ride-or-die chick at that time. We did so much in ministry; she was considered my sister. She would always say to me, "Lori, you're going to be in the family one day," and I would laugh and say, "Oh yeah, I'm sure I will be one day."

Then it happened, the call came July 14, 2017, in the quietness of my home and life, little did I know the peace that I had would begin a downhill spiral, and the gates of hell would open. I checked my phone; there were three missed calls. So what do we do as curious women? We pick up the phone and call the number back. On the receiving end was the man that I had fallen in love with so many years ago. I thought God had finally answered my prayers. You see, for ten years, God had kept me in the quietness of my home and raising my children. I began to talk on the phone and listen to this young man, this preacher that I've known for so long. Despite the warnings from my children, they told me, "Do not get involved,

Mom." I didn't listen; for me, it was an answered prayer. How many know the devil can answer prayers too? This awesome man of God, preacher, prophet, dressed nice, would come into town and speak at my friend's church. He would speak so eloquently, the Word of the Lord. He was my friend's cousin. How many of you know that the gifts and calling come without repentance? So on July 14, 2017, I called this young man back. He said his birthday was July 21, 2017. He said in conversation with me he had been walking out in the yard and praying, talking with the Lord, and said he was ready for his wife. He, at the time, was living in Greenville, Mississippi. He said I was his queen, he said I was his wife, and he said I was the one. He asked me would I take a trip to Greenville, Mississippi, and spend the weekend with him for his birthday. That was the following weekend. Despite the warning from my children, I did not listen.

How many know that warning comes before destruction? Proverbs 6:18, "Pride goes before destruction, and a haughty spirit before a fall." So I prepared to go to Greenville, Mississippi, and on July 21, 2017, on his birthday, a trap was set in the form of intimacy. God had kept me for ten years, and in a split second, the ten years had gone down the drain. You see, one month prior, in a phone call, a very dear sister of mine, who was very strong with prophetic insight, said to me, "God is not going to release you to date until your baby girl Savannah turns eighteen." So he and I talked on the phone almost daily. The following weekend my baby would turn eighteen. So he put plans in motion to come to me. He said he wanted to come and spend the following weekend with me; it was then going to be my daughter's birthday. July 30, she would turn eighteen. He traveled up from Greenville, Mississippi, and we sat, and we had dinner; it was great. She turned eighteen; it was wonderful.

That weekend, I moved him in. Everything that I stood for, everything that I believed in, I no longer stood for and believed in. It was as if I put God on the shelf or on the back burner. I knew better; however, I thought this man was my husband, this was an answered prayer, the preacher prophet that God had finally sent to me. On September 5, 2017, we got married; we never had traditional counseling, we just went and got married. This was a man of God; my prayers were answered, or so I thought. We married in Marion, Arkansas, in a dark, dingy file room; there were no other rooms available for us. Five people in attendance: my mom, his dad, my daughter, myself, my husband, and the woman that facilitated our marriage. God spoke to me then and said, "Daughter, the head is not the covering, and the covering is not the head." God was warning me then. But I was already in it, so for the next thirty-six months, I would go through hell in the form of drinking, drugging, and gambling. He would be away three and four days at a time. My husband, preacher, prophet, man of God, gifts, and calling come without repentance; however, there was an agenda. So much darkness, so much baggage came into the marriage.

In March 2020, I could no longer handle the thirty-six months of my life spinning out of control. I had relocated to another city where the family is now living in Cincinnati, Ohio. The baggage from Tennessee filtered over. I had a brand-new job started fresh January 7, 2019. I was living in a house with my son, which he purchased. My baby girl, his sister, was attending college in Wilmington, Ohio. My son was working in Kroger; things were well for the most part, yet my husband took the baggage from one state to the next. So the drinking and drugging continued, even though we were in another state. To be exact, we were doing good as a family, yet my husband's life was spinning out of control, and he did not see it, and it was hell for the most part. The family suffered. I stood and watched this man of God that I loved so much kill himself slowly.

So on March 6, 2020, I decided to drive him back to Memphis because I could not handle anymore. I felt that he could be with his family since he was very deeply attached to them. However, to our surprise, nobody wanted to deal with him or wanted to help. The family he was so very attached to wanted nothing to do with the issues. I can remember my son, Asa, standing in the house of my husband's uncle Eric, who since God has called home, and saying to him, "Pop, do you really want to change? Is this something that you want to do?" My husband looked up at him and said, "Son, I'll do my best." I looked at my husband and said, "You cannot do your best; you have to want to make an intelligent decision and want to change your life forever." He looked at me and said, "Yes, I do want to change. I finally want to change. I no longer want to be like this." So we brought him back to Cincinnati. On March 6, he made the decision to change his life. On March 7, 2020, he went in for detox. This was in Kentucky, and on March 13, 2020, one week later, he was flown to Jacksonville, Florida, where he would start his recovery process.

We conferenced while he was there; it was a crazy time. It was the start of the Covid pandemic. At that time, my job transitioned me home to work. Things seemed like they were going crazy. However, there was finally a plan in place. Forty-five days into his recovery, my phone rang; he said he was ready to come home; he was completed. I was not ready for him to come home; who was this man? All I knew was someone full of substance. At the present day, he has been clean and sober for twenty-nine months.

As I write the final chapter to my book, today is August 15, 2022. On September 5, 2022, we will be married for five years. In the beginning, I told God I would give it five years. The Lord said to me, "Get him where he needs to be." I've done everything required of me; my assignment is now completed. I have to decide: Do I want to stay in the trap that was originally set for me five years ago, or do I want to finally close the chapter of this book and move forward in freedom?

RECAP AND FINAL REFLECTION

I often wonder why my book, completed in 2010, was never published. It was because seven years later, from the completion of the seventh chapter of the book, would be the final chapter, number eight. In 2017, I had to walk through an experience, the final trap that the devil had set before me. I can honestly say now I am walking in the freeness, fullness, and wholeness of God. I am set free from all the snares and the cycles that the enemy had in store for me. You see, the man that I thought was my husband was just my assignment.

My husband is very loving; he's very kind; he loves hard; he is a protector, and sometimes he could be so overbearing that he smothers me to the point he pushes you away.

I can never be just me; he would never allow me to just be me. There would always be questions or why I am doing a certain thing. I could never drive my own car because he wanted to drive for me. I could never go do my nails or my hair or get my eyes done because he wanted to sit there and be with me all the time. I can remember being in the car while he's driving, and I'm just looking off in a daze, feeling depressed, not wanting to be in the present situation.

You see, I believe that God brought us to a five-year full circle. As I look back, the dates coincide with five years ago, in 2017, including the present day or shall I say, year 2022. It's something to think about or even reflect on. Five years ago, it was a moment of passion, and then planning for my baby girl's birthday dinner. That was the day that my husband's longtime friend, Bishop mentor, had released him to be with me. Present day, we finally had our first vacation; baby girl's birthday was spent in West Palm Beach, Florida. Once again, the dates coincide exactly. We were to fly home on July

31, 2022. We arrived in Southaven, Mississippi, once again to meet his longtime mentor friend. This is a man my husband looked up to and has known for many years. However, the flight was canceled in Atlanta, Georgia, pushing the arrival date one day forward. In reflecting, I see if the flight had not been canceled, we would have arrived in South Haven, Mississippi, on the same date of my daughter's birthday, five years ago. I say once again, the dates coincide from past to present, and my father God in heaven has literally set the clock back. My husband would always say and make this statement, "There's a reaping and a sowing that needs to take place." God did that, not man. Now is the time of reflection, redemption, forgiveness, and repentance to take place. We are now present day in a five-week separation for the most part. Or shall I say, for the moment, I believe that God is doing a reset. He was staying with a longtime mentor, a bishop friend, in Greenville, Mississippi, five years ago, and present day, he is in Greenville, Mississippi, with his mentor, a longtime friend.

So I pose the question not only to myself but to those that will soon be reading this book: Do you want to continue to stay in the trap that was set before you in your past, or do you close the final chapter? Or do you stay on the course and continue with the assignment?

The choice is yours. It's up to you. Repent, go to God, get back up. Remember, the earth is not our home; we are just passing through.

WOMEN OF LIGHT

> The thief cometh not, but for to steal, and to kill,
> and to destroy: I am come that they might have life,
> and that they might have it more abundantly.
> —John 10:10

You are now in a season where the Lord wants you to come out of your dark area and press back into the light. God has shown me in my prayer time and study that we as women, from time to time, have allowed people to come in and crush us. They have tried to steal our self-worth, whether it be a husband, boyfriend, sister, brother, cousins, or family members; this list can go on and on. Your self-worth, somewhere along the way, has been stolen from you. It is now time for you to be redeemed by the Lord.

I am here to tell you, woman of light—and the reason why I call you woman of light is that the darkness of your life is no more—it's time to rise up and rebuild your wall that might have fallen. However, it's time to get back up and start rebuilding that wall (*Nehemiah 1:3–4*). The Eternal Wall represents *the strength of God*.

We all have diaries, dark secrets; they are called the "Dear diary" moments. So here we go, let's go down memory lane. Now keep in mind, this sister sharing has come from the darkness. The Lord has healed me and delivered me. I am now free in Jesus. He has commissioned me now to impart hope into the lives of his children, and yes, you are one of God's chosen children. Amen. So now, let us talk. Yes, I was that woman; my self-worth was stolen, not only by one but by several people. Now let us keep in mind, we are not here to smash the brothers; God loves them too.

Yes, my self-worth was stolen, and I could not share with anyone. I was a Christian woman, walking the walk and talking the talk; however, my walking was all alone. I was drowning in despair, could not share with my momma or friends, 'cause they would say things like I was crazy. So I would walk, and I would talk, and I would put a big smile on my face and go home, and behind closed doors, I was living in hell. I would cook dinner, and if it did not smell right or taste right, I was slapped in the face, kicked to the floor; my self-worth was slowly being stolen from me. Remember, I come from experience, so let us continue to share some more "Dear diary" moments. Then you're asked into the bedroom and expected to perform like nothing ever happened; your self-worth was being stolen. You're smashed in the head with a brick or stabbed in the shoulder and being left for dead. Then, when you think it's all over, the nightmares are gone, and you're free, your house goes up in flames. Everything you've built up, all your hard work, gone, no more. Your self-worth stolen, no more. You're lying in ruins; the wall has come down, crashing down. You feel like all hope is gone, nothing left, gloom, despair. "Why me? Why is this happening to me?" And you start to question yourself, "What have I done wrong? Why are my cycles repeating? Why am I still attracting a certain element? Why do I keep getting pushed deeper and deeper in the mud?"

Say out loud with me, "No more will this happen to me. I have just been set free in Jesus."

> For God so loved the world that he gave his only begotten son, then whosoever believe it in him should not perish, but have everlasting life. (John 3:16)

Okay, sisters of light, I rose, and you will rise too. I rose because there were sisters like me who had already gone through and came along the way, encouraged me, and gave me a message of hope. So now, I'm sharing hope with you. This is your season and time to start out, start rebuilding your wall. No more will you be crushed, smashed, kicked to the ground. The Lord loves you; you have been created in His image, and you are victorious. You are a beautiful sister. Start doing self-confessions. Talk to yourself; say the words, "I am somebody. I am fearfully and wonderfully made in the image of God." Continue to confess that daily. Say to yourself, "I'm whole and complete. Amen."

I now stand. I am whole and complete in God. I am a treasure of self-worth, and so are you.

> Teach me your way, LORD, that I may rely on
> your faithfulness; give me an undivided heart,
> that I may fear your name. (Psalm 86:11)

Rise, my sister of light. This sister is praying for you, along with a team that God has assigned to do ministry. We are praying for your deliverance. If you are in a relationship that is not healthy, come out this day to be free. No more will your self-worth be stolen from you. This is your day to walk in the freedom in the Lord and be set free.

If you are unchurched, allow the Lord to direct you to a local church. You cannot do this alone. And tell them about your decision.

I pray that you have been changed, encouraged, and blessed by the reading of this word.

Prophetess Lori A. Manson Futrell
Founder of Vision of Purpose Ministries
Original version 2007, reaffirmed 2022

IT'S TIME TO RISE UP

> For I know the plans I have for you, says the Lord. They are plans of good and not of evil, to give you a future hope. In those days when you pray, I will listen you will find me when you seek me, if you look for me earnest.
> —Jeremiah 29:11–13

I recently had the opportunity to have a conversation with someone very close to me within the ministry. We spoke about race and culture. How we, being people of color growing up, have had word curses spoken over our lives. People have tried to speak harshly over us and what the Lord has called us to do. But I've come to realize that I know a savior named Jesus, and if you know him like I do, you too have now become whole and complete in his image. This is why we must, from time to time, refer to the scripture, and I say, "I know the plans God has for me; they are good and not of evil. Amen." We are more than conquerors in Christ Jesus. Fellow Christians, you are the head and not the tail; you look high and not low. Your help does not come from below, but it comes from above. Men of God, you will rise up. Sisters of God, it's time for you to rise up. No more will you be tossed to and fro. Repeat this after me: "Today is my day to be set free in Jesus's name."

To the single-parent families, no more will you be called dysfunctional, whether you are a man or woman. It's time for you to rise up and walk in the calling of the Lord. You do not have to be a pulpit minister; we all have been called to a certain area of our lives. Perhaps God wants to use you to break generational curses. We all have been called to that one certain area; God is waiting on you.

Now, to my sisters, it's time that we rise up. Stop sitting around on your pity party, allowing life to pass you by, feeling sorry for yourself. You must be consistent and constant in the Lord. Refer to the scripture, for he knows the plans he has for you. Sometimes we think it's not fair; you may have children that have gone astray, doing everything that is not in the will of God. Well, what are you going to do about it? Are you going to complain, or are you going to be consistent in your prayers? Press in, press through, lay before the father, lay out if you need to, cry out to him. (What does the scripture say? "In those days when you pray, he will listen.") Not when you feel like praying, it's when you pray.

Once again, I'm speaking to my sisters; I must have a heart-to-heart and become transparent. I too have a daughter of destiny out there doing any and everything that is not in the will of the father. I have no problem laying out before the father, praying, pressing, putting that plate down, and believing for her total salvation and deliverance. She does not struggle with one demon but many. She is a daughter of destiny, a daughter of Zion; she is preparing a major testimony. I hold fast to the promise of the Lord. This is for both men and women of God; you must trust the Lord for your children. And at the appointed time, they will be free. For his promises, yes and amen. No, it's not easy, and yet at times, it does get hard, but you still must hold fast to God's promises. You are not alone. You must press into the Lord. The problem is, we've allowed busyness to come into our lives. God forbid we lay out before the Lord. Well, newsflash, it's time to get back down on your knees, lay out before the Lord. We must be consistent in God. Society has adapted to a miracle-in-a-box, microwave generation, when God is saying it's all or nothing.

To my sisters and my brothers, we must rise up, press back, go down into the enemy's camp, take back what the enemy has stolen from us. It's time to stand. Is your spouse unsaved? Rise up; you must lead by example. Does your spouse see Jesus in you? Are you really giving him a reason to come out of the pit? Or are you always complaining? Love is the key; that is the Lord's greatest gift. Stop expecting people to feel sorry for you. It's time to rise up. God has given you boldness and authority in him. Once again, refer to the scripture, for God knows the plans he has for you, plans of good and not of evil.

My sisters and brothers, when you feel you are in a downhill spiral, hold to the Lord. He is your anchor, your foundation. Find a prayer partner; you must have accountability. It's time for you to rise up and walk out the plans and the process the Lord has for you. Stop tipping the hand of the Lord and seek his face. Time out for instant fixes; God does not work that way. To achieve your destiny, it's going to take work. You must be consistent in your praise. The Lord can and will give you the desires of your heart. The key is you seeking his face, not tipping his hand. Are you willing to speak to that mountain and say, "Be now removed," or are you just going to settle where you are? Your mind belongs to God; stop allowing the enemy to come in and torment your mind. We so many times want to blame each other. We need to start seeing ourselves from who we really are. *Do not be afraid to ask God to fix you.*

Once again, refer to your scripture, for he knows the plans for you, says the Lord. Amen. You cannot abort the plan and the process the Lord has for you. Myself, when my home was burned to the ground and everything was stolen, I never aborted the plan God had for me. I stayed consistent in him. I had to grab hold like never before; my life depended on the Lord, and he was my comforter, he was my strong tower, and he was my provider. That scripture had become engrafted in my soul. God had me in a position that I could not call on anybody else but him. Storms of life are not easy, but if you keep driving, God will take you through them.

We as Christians, when everything is going fine, we praise him, we pray to him, we even go to church, having fellowship with one another. But when tragedy comes, we tend to run far from God instead of running to the Lord. We have it all wrong when the Lord is saying seek him while he may be found. God is not a temporary God. God does not want to be temporary in your life; he is not someone that you put in a box or on a shelf and call on him when you're in trouble. He is almighty, and he wants to be permanent and engrafted in your spirit.

God is always there to meet you at your point of need, with his arms open wide. *Revelations 3:20, tells us, "Behold, I stand at the door and knock."* God will not enter in until you open the door.

There is a clarion call that I am sending out to all my brothers and sisters in the Lord. Men of God, it's time to man up. Women of God, it's time to rise up. Time to go forth and reach the lost communities set before us that are lying in ruins.

This is for my brothers: it's time for you to take your rightful place. You are the authority; you are the head and not the tail. The Lord has made you the head for a reason. Now keep in mind, my brothers, we as sisters in Christ are also rising up. No more will we allow the devil to wreak havoc in our homes and in our communities. We are behind you and beside you to do what needs to be done, not for self-glory but for the glory of the Lord.

No more will the devil come in and confuse or consume your minds with doubt. No more will you be deceived with your finances. God has given you a plan, and he will prosper you. God has now given you clear vision. No more will you have blurry tunnel vision; you will no longer look to the left nor to the right; you will now move forward and only see Jesus.

This is your year to walk in overflow. This is your year for your family. This is your year for your financial breakthrough. This is your year for more of the Lord. I declare and decree it in the name of the Lord Jesus, and I seal it with the blood of him. Amen.

I thank the Lord for every path he has allowed me to go down. If it had not been for the Lord by my side, I would not be who I am today.

My prayer is that you will apply to your life what thus says the Lord, sons of Abraham and daughters of Sarah. Stand up and take your rightful place in the kingdom of God.

This is your year of overflow. Allow the presence of our Lord and Savior Jesus Christ to overflow in and through your life.

Prophetess Lori A. Manson Futrell
Founder of Vision of Purpose Ministries
Original version 2007, reaffirmed 2022

CONCLUSION

For me, it's a new beginning. We arrived in Memphis on June 6, 2010. When you obey God, everything that was lost can and will be restored to you. The key to this Christian walk is repentance and to trust and obey the Lord.

I have just taken you through a twenty-year journey. I am now sixty-four and satisfied with Jesus. My life is now complete. I am saved, sanctified, filled with the Holy Ghost, washed in the blood of Jesus, created in his image, anointed and appointed for the master's use. For greater is he who is within me than he who is within the world. Remember, the eyes of the Lord are everywhere.

For my readers, you must get to the place in life where you say, "It's me, oh Lord, standing in the need of prayer. It's me, oh Lord, standing in the need of guidance. It's me, oh Lord, standing in the need of instruction. It's me, oh Lord, I surrender all to you, and I now stop running." (For me, my running days are over.)

The Bible declares in Matthew 20:16, "So the last shall be first, and the first shall be last." Many are called, but few are chosen.

I have made it through the refining process. I stand before you whole and complete.

The son I spoke about, Art, who in the beginning of the writing of this book had an identity crisis, is now whole and complete. He is married to a wonderful young lady named Lorraine Marie. He is a business owner and a graphic designer.

The daughter, Shannon, I spoke about in the beginning of the writing of this book, who was running, is now on her way back to Jesus, focusing on the Lord and putting her life into perspective.

The son Asa I spoke about in the beginning of the writing of this book has completed trade school. He has now been working for Kroger for ten plus years. He is also living in his second home purchased, where I reside with him.

My baby girl, whom I spoke about in the beginning of the writing of this book, is still whole and complete, loving the Lord Jesus with all her might, mind, body, heart, and soul. She is in her final year of college at Wilmington College, Ohio. She is studying, and she will soon receive her bachelor's degree in Biology in health science. She also holds many leadership titles within the college. She is hardworking, but most of all, she truly loves the Lord and people.

Oh, and for me, loving, learning, and leaning on Jesus is a daily PROCESS.

The Bible shares in the book of *Romans 10:9*, *"If you confess with your mouth the Lord Jesus and believe in your heart that God had raised him from the dead, you will be saved." It's a simple confession. Verse 10, "For with the heart, one believes unto righteousness, and with the mouth, confession is made unto salvation."*

My prayer for you is that the reading of this book has blessed you. Continue to pray for me, and soon I will be coming to a city near you. Prior to the close and the completion of this book, I heard the Lord say

> But they that wait upon the Lord shall renew their strength; they shall mount up with wings of Eagles; They shall run, and not be weary; and they shall walk, and faint not. (Isaiah 40:31)

Then I heard the Lord say, "Because you have waited on me, this is your eagle-flying season. You will fly high, and you will soar for me because you have waited."

This book was completed at the age of fifty and now reaffirmed for a timely seasonal release. I am now sixty-four.

May the Lord bless and keep my readers always.

The Value Of Process

$\mathcal{P}$ - You must *Pray*
1 Thessalonians 5: 17 Pray without ceasing

$\mathcal{R}$ - You are *Redeemed*
Revelation 12: 11 And they overcame him by the blood of the Lamb, and by the word of their testimony

$\mathcal{O}$ - You are an *Overcomer*
Philippians 4:13 I can do all things through Christ which strengthens me

$\mathcal{C}$ - You must be *Committed* and consistent with Christ
Galatians 2:20 a - I am crucified with Christ: never theless I live: yet not I, but Christ livith in

$\mathcal{E}$ - You have *Everlasting* life
John 3: 16 For God so loved the world he gave his only begotten son whom ever believes in him shall not parish but have everlasting life.

$\mathcal{S}$ - You must be willing to *Sacrifice* for the Christ
Romans 12:1 I BESEECH you therefore, brethren, by the mercies of God, that you present your bodies as a living sacrifice, holy, acceptable unto God which is your reasonable service

$\mathcal{S}$ - You are *Saved* by grace
Romans 10: 9 That if thou shall confess with thy mouth the Lord Jesus and believe in thine heart that God hath raised him from the dead thou shall be saved

Through Teaching we apply, through application we are Trained through Training we become Transformed

ABOUT THE AUTHOR

Prophetess Lori A. Manson Futrell

She is a woman of excellence, purpose, and vision.

The founder of Vision of Purpose Ministries, Int., she is a graduate of NCCT, North Carolina College of Theology, Carolina Beach, North Carolina. While there, she obtained her degrees in both theology and biblical learning. She has an associate's and bachelor's degree, completed in June 2007.

Prophetess Lori A. Manson Futrell looks back at her time in school as just a closer walk with the Father. She also received her certification from the Woman-to-Woman Mentoring Institute, Darlene McCarty Ministries, Cathedral of Praise, Cordova, Tennessee, in February of 2007 and 2008.

She also received her certificate of ministry license on July 22, 2017, at International Women's Ministry Alliance Incorporated, Houston, Texas, from Dr. D. Tyler Brown, apostle.

Prophetess Lori A. Manson Futrell was born in Port Chester, New York, on October 28, 1959, and grew up in Connecticut. She accepted the Lord Jesus Christ in her life while she was pregnant with her second son, Asa, in March of 1990. In May of 1998, the prophet relocated to Memphis-Millington, Tennessee. In April 2001, she received her calling into the ministry.

On June 26, 2008, she relocated to Houston, Texas, for a two-year season with her two youngest children. While there, she served under the leadership and direction of Reginald DeVaughn Sr., pastor of Silverlake Church, located in Pearland, Texas. On June 1, 2010, her season ended; she was released and relocated back to the Memphis, Tennessee, area.

She is no stranger to the kingdom of God. She is a believer in the Word; she believes that knowledge is power when it comes to Kingdom dominion. Since being saved, Father God has done an accelerated work in her life. Prophetess Lori operates under a five-fold ministry.

Some have called her a minister to many ministries, and it is said she has a shepherd's heart. She has been given the opportunity to have many sons and daughters within the ministry as she continues to teach, train, and transform the lives of individuals.

In the early morning hours of April 1, 2007, Prophetess Lori received her worldwide mandate from the Lord, saying, "Tell my people to draw unto me. Sound the *Trumpet of Warning*. Tell them the time is soon of my return." She has become a true prophet to the nations. She travels, teaches, and preaches when called upon. Some have called her a modern-day Jeremiah.

Prophetess Lori A. Manson Futrell currently resides in the city of Cincinnati with her two younger children, Savannah Faith and Asa Eugene. She is currently under the leadership and direction of Pastor Eric and Kim Petree, Citygate Church (Forest Park Location).